T0380954

HELP ME, I'M IN FOSTER CARE

A Guide from Seven Letters for Families and Caretakers of Children in "the System"

TENIO S. COUSIN, MA

ISBN: Softcover   978-1-9845-4467-4
         EBook   978-1-9845-4466-7

Print information available on the last page

Rev. date: 08/01/2018

To order additional copies of this book, contact:
Xlibris
1-888-795-4274
www.Xlibris.com
Orders@Xlibris.com

HELP ME,
I'M IN FOSTER CARE

*A Guide from Seven Letters for Families and
Caretakers of Children in "the System"*

-Letters are based on true stories and actual events-

BY: TENIO S. COUSIN, MA

HELP ME, I'M IN FOSTER CARE

A Guide from Seven Letters for Families and
Caretakers of Children in "the System"

BY: TENIO S. COUSIN, MA

Dedicated to my son Tray K. Coppola
I have always loved you more than my own life!

FROM THE AUTHOR:

As a person who has experienced many differing roles dealing with children that are "in the system," I have grown to learn and understand the frustrations that challenge the homes of foster and adoptive families alike. Many times we setup services to aid children in care; however, we fail to recognize the fact that the instant they enter a family as a child in care, that family's entire unit is affected as well. The mom, dad, children, extended family, church, and even pets undergo life altering events. I am utilizing this book to tell their stories, their cries, their pains, their joys, their wishes, and their needs in the form of letters.

This book is a collection of letters written from differing perspectives of working with "children in care." It is common to hear the story of foster care from a foster child's perspective. I believe this is absolutely necessary. However, I also believe there are some key components that are left out. The story from the other side also needs to be told. The story from those who help foster children need to be validated so that a full and accurate picture is painted. I hope this book helps the state, the nation, and the world recognize a little better the true dynamics of our foster and adoptive families. If we are to truly have "the best interest of our children in mind," we must understand the TRUE needs of their temporary support systems as well. We must truly assist them in maintaining and improving the quality of life for these children but not at the expense of decreasing and or devaluing the quality of life for the caretakers involved.

I don't think that value comes from the monetary per diem provided by the state. I'm not declaring this book as a fix it to all the problems of the foster system. I am simply providing an aspect to consider as we strive to find clarity in the well-being of our kids.

Table of Contents

FROM THE MOTHER

Dear Listener,

I don't know where to start. My entire life has been turned inside out. I don't sleep at all, and I have more responsibilities than I've ever encountered in my life. I don't think you realize what is happening to me. Let me walk you through my day.

I get up at 5:00a.m., because I have to have ALL of my kids ready for the bus by 6:30a.m. Now I don't mean just my biological kids, but I am also talking about the new foster kids in my home. You see a mom always includes everyone in the count but herself. I'd like to say that I told the kids to get up, and they did, however, that would definitely be the Leave it to Beaver's version of my story. No, I walked in and said, "Get up." My oldest child, biological that is, woke up crying. I tried to talk to her about it but before I could get out the wrong in "What's wrong," I heard a loud, "Fuck You, Bitch" across the hall. Ignoring the fact that my daughter still needed me, I left her and ran across the hall to redirect the problem.

I walked in and asked, "What happened?"

"Jack pissed in the bed, and now I smell like him," was John's cry. Jack and John are our new foster kids. They've been here for about four months now.

"Just give me the sheets and take a shower John. Jack, you wait right here."
I tried to talk to Jack, but he ran out the room, up the hall way, and out of the house. I think I looked thirty minutes for that child before I found him behind a bush outside. Suddenly the bus drove up. Instantly, I realized that I didn't finish talking to my daughter. I have no idea where John is or what he has on, and Jack is still unprepared. "Come on Jack, it's ok!" My daughter raced out the door.

I told her, "We'll talk this afternoon Hun!"

"Forget it Mother, I'm ok," She yelled back.

As if that wasn't enough, my husband sped out the drive way for work. I'm sure he is upset because he says I never give him anytime either. I looked back at Jack. He had a smirk on his face and said,

"It looks like dad's angry again."

I took Jack and John to school. The cell phone rang at least five times every half-hour. One call was Jack's school telling me about his suspension because of a fight the other day. Another call was his caseworker telling me that as a foster parent, I needed to have him at his family visit by four. The day continued on like this. Calls continued seemingly on the hour. I argued with my husband on every break he had, and my daughter shut herself up refusing to talk to me when she got home. When I discipline the children, my husband says I'm too harsh, especially with Jack. He says, I should just lay off. Naturally, Jack smiles about all of those arguments. Jack really needs a spanking, especially after spitting on me and kicking my ankle, but he knows that's out of the question.

"I'll tell, if you touch me."

Now of course you know this means I go ahead a spank him – hoping he does tell. Maybe they will move him and end this night mare. I don't have the heart to put him out myself, but this could be a way. Crazy thing is that doesn't work either. He never tells, and I am still frustrated. Looks like its back to the drawing board. Between cooking, cleaning, washing, ironing, and being at everyone's beckoning call, I am a step from insane.

"Isn't that all mothers?" you say.

"No!"

All mothers don't clean up pee every morning from the 13 year old. They don't get five calls a day from the teacher, principal, caseworker, probation officer, and extended family to complain about the many wrong doings committed by her children.

My husband wants to leave because he feels neglected. My body hurts from the constant kicks and hits; my eyes hurt from the lack of sleep, and my head hurts from the continued exposure to it! If I cry it out, I'm being too emotional. If I close it up, I need help. I don't feel much these days. I use to look forward to vacation. Now it's just a count down to when I return to hell. My resting stops are juvenile court, the psychologist office, mental health, DFCS, the grocery store, and the school. I'm tired, broken, and misunderstood. I Quit.

Always,
An Abused Mother

From the Father

Dear Listener,

    I don't really know what to do. This was my wife's idea anyways. I never got that attached to the whole foster care idea. Ok, I admit it. I did think about the money, and it seemed like a pretty easy job to me. However, opposite to popular belief, all people don't do it for the money. Trust me when I say, It just isn't worth it. If I had known my family was going to end up like this, I would have never made this commitment. Let me explain what I mean.

    My daughter never talks to us anymore. She just goes to her room or tries to spend the night away from home a lot. I never see my wife. I miss her hugs, her kisses, her smiles, her food, and her touch. Most of the time she says she's tired. We can't have a full conversation without the phone ringing every five minutes. I don't remember what her kisses feel like. I can't remember the last time our family had a dinner where the meal didn't end with a fight. My house smells like urine. I get up 3 to 4 times a night just to check on the safety of my family. There is something about that Jack that scares me. The caseworkers and counselors all say it's normal, and he's getting help for it. They minimize the problem and treat us as if we are stupid. They tell us we have to take classes just to learn parenting skills for "their children."

    I was going to tell my wife that I might loose my job because the schools keep calling me. I can't work like this too much longer. I know my wife thinks that I have no clue about her needs. I don't know it all, but I see she is under constant pressure. I want to do something, but she keeps me out.

If that little Jack bows up at me one more time, I swear he's mine. The money's ok, but not good enough to destroy my family over. I don't think I can take too much more of this not seeing my wife and watching her suffer all the same time.

My child looks depressed. I never meant to bring this into her childhood like this. I know she just wants to help mommy and daddy, but that's not her job. She should be playing, laughing, and enjoying these years.

I swear if I get one more call, one more sleepless night, one more complaint by a caseworker, one more rejection by my wife, one more stress headache, one more anything, I Quit. It's funny. You go into this as a helper. You offer the state your home, your family, your life so that another life lives, and the result you get is total chaos. People talk down to you. You have to prove your worth as an individual again. It's as if your reputation goes right out the door. These kids come in and tell stories about your family that never existed before. It seems like the workers and counselors believe them all. Suddenly you find yourself proving you are not abusive, negligent, or harmful. You begin to question how safe you can keep your family if these stories are bought so easily. Overnight you go from being a reputable citizen to a man questioned of integrity, of honor, of maturity, and of heart. Is it really worth all of this?

Sincerely,
A distressed Father

FROM THE CHILDREN

Dear Mom and Dad,

Do we have to keep doing this? I don't mean to sound selfish, but I hate those kids. Please send them back. Why do we have to take care of them? Don't they have their own parents? They take all of your time. I have to share everything I have. If I have a question about school or even a problem, I can't ask it. All your time is spent scolding Jack and John. All we ever do is drive to those stupid meetings. We go to shrinks all the time. Strange people come in and out of our house looking through all of our things. I know that little brat is stealing my stuff and hiding it. Furthermore, he's a liar. It seems like you believe everything he says. I know you have to see he's just starting trouble.

Look at our walls. There are holes everywhere. Our house used to be pretty. Now there are ink marks everywhere. The furniture is broken. The windows are cracked. Our car smells like urine, and I can't sleep at night. My grades are going down and you don't even notice. Do you know that I won an award for student of the month? It's kind of crazy. I could fail every class right now, and I don't think you would even see it. You think that would be a child's greatest pleasure, but it isn't. Not when it goes un-noticed for so long that you no longer feel you exist. I hate to be lectured and go on and on, so I won't. But you should know that I am hurting, crying, angry, and I miss my family. I don't mean to sound selfish, but I want MY family back. Please send those kids away. I miss you mom and dad. I want us to be happy again. Instead all we do is fight. No one really talks anymore. We don't do anything fun. We don't have anything that is ours anymore. Maybe I should go to foster care. I don't get my family anymore either, but no one seems to care. Everyone is doing everything for them. What about me? Do I still get to be loved? Do I still matter? This makes a kid want to quit.

I love you,
Your Child

From the Extended Family

Dear Listener,

What has happened to our family?

Extended Member 1:
We don't know what to do. Sometimes it seems like they are way too harsh on those kids. They are always in trouble. They can't go anywhere without an adult. We don't want to intrude, but it just seems like the kids just need a little love. Look at what they've been through. Who could ask anything more?

Extended Member 2:
Those kids are crazy. Every time they come to my house something is out of place. They steal, and they torment my kids. I just hope they don't come back. I'm sorry. I love my sister, her husband, and my niece, but I can't take that little demon.

Extended Member 3:
Somebody needs to beat their little asses. DFCS has messed those kids up!

Extended Member 4:
What the hell?

Extended Member 5:
We use to get together all the time. We use to laugh, play, and run together. Now all they do is doctor's visits, counseling appointments, and meetings. I miss them so much

Extended Member 6:
Why don't they just give 'em back? I know they love them. I know their heart is in it, but I can't stand seeing them like this and not being able to do a thing about it. They are imprisoned in their own homes. They can't stay at any family functions for too long, and they never smile anymore. They look so tired. Their eyes are always full of water. The whole family shuts down when they are around. No one knows if it's ok to joke, laugh, play, or cry. We fear that we may say the wrong thing, provoke the wrong thoughts, or make life that much more difficult. I hope that child knows that they have given up everything they call family for them. It all seems so unfair. Do they really get anything out of it? I'd quit. It just doesn't seem worth it.

Extended Member 7:
Here they come. Hurry up ya'll, let's go!

See What I mean.

Sincerely,
The Extended Family

From the Professionals

Dear Listener:

What was I thinking going into this field? 52, 23, and 58 are my new best friends. "What are those?" you ask. I will tell you. The first number is the number of kids I am responsible for. Now I know they don't live in my home, but let me tell you it isn't peaceful at night knowing that 28 of my kids have a 75% chance of disrupting by the end of the night, and I am going to have to find them placement in a county that doesn't seem to have a surplus of foster home placements. 23 is the number of visits I made today. Half of those visits involved trying to get families to keep kids. The other half involved arguing with new intakes and schools. That other 58 is the number of calls I actually returned. Now you know that means I am going to get cussed out for not returning the other 80 who demanded that I call them immediately. It's funny how they all expect me to call all them immediately. They don't seem to understand the impossibility in this. They all yell at me, if I take more than five hours calling them back. Furthermore, I get classified as a poor caseworker. The kids call me at least 12 times within an hour and I end up explaining to my supervisor the fact that I could never answer all those demands in the time limit that they all give me.

My family is mad at me too. My husband never sees me. My son says I give everybody else's child my time too. I have a family too, and I am tired. If I don't call immediately, it's not personal. If I fudge the truth a little to make a placement, forgive me, but again, I'm tired and I want to go to my family like you do. I don't mean to make your life difficult, but I got to place this child, so I left out what I judged to be the least amount of information I could give without being completely false. I am trying. I am on child number 34 of 52. I know you need a case plan. I know they need a doctor's visit. I know you've left me 12 messages, and I know you're house is in a wreck. I'm trying damn it! Give me a second. Multiply your child placement by 20 more kids, 50 more calls, and 80 more unpleased customers and hopefully you will have a little mercy. Forgive me this time, and be patient enough to know that I'm doing a job no one else wanted. I'm doing a service no one else has the time or monetary means to commit to (including me), and I'm trying real hard not to quit. I know I chose the job, but give me a little credit for attempt to perform a "good" service.

Patiently working,
The Professional

P.S. Yea, I know you spanked them, but let's face it. We both know they are not being abused, there is no where for them to go, and quite frankly, they needed it. I support and need you more than I think you think I realize.

From The Church

Dear Listener,

I know you think we are the biggest hypocrites alive. I don't know what to say. I have never had to ask a family not to bring guest. Usually the church opens its doors to everyone. I still feel a terrible amount of guilt about it sometimes, but what else can you do? This family brought a child here that I am sure needed some type of exorcism ritual. The child yells out in class. He hits the other students. He wipes his nose on all the bibles and song books. He turns on the gas stove and threatens to blow the building up. He yells and laughs out during the sermon. He says sexually inappropriate comments to the people in our church. He curses out the Sunday school teacher, and then he laughs. He clogs all the toilets, and he turns over the trash cans. Did I mention that he drank all the communion juice and ate the bread too?

I'd like to say this happens once a quarter, but in truth this happens two or three times every Sunday. My members are complaining. People are leaving and refusing to return or bring their children to be exposed to this chaos at church. We are constantly paying for repairs to books, windows, and furniture in the church.

The final blow came when I found the child with marijuana. He was smoking it in the bathroom, and he was trying to give it out to other children. I had to make a decision. I could not allow God's house to be mocked in such a way, so I asked the family to remove the child from campus. I know you say we are supposed to be all loving, kindhearted, forgiving, and long suffering. We really try and follow that example. Please don't judge us when we simply attempt to bring peace to God's house. We don't judge you as a parent or foster parent. We are not sure nor are we aware of the initiation of this child's problems. We can offer some services, but we must protect the safety of our members. We think the role you are taking is noble and well deserving of honor, but we must provide a worship atmosphere that is fair to all. Your child has changed the dynamics of our worship. He has changed the relationship of individuals in the church. Some want to help. Others want him gone. Arguments and splits have occurred in the battle of doing "what is right." I can't help but feel as a pastor that I wish you had never brought this child to us. May God have mercy on me as I feel hypocritical for saying that. I know we are all sinners saved by grace, but do you completely stop the saving of all else for this one? Such judgment calls should not be made or ever have to be experienced. I will never forget the pain this has caused. I ask God to guide this congregation and all congregations alike in managing this evil scheme of the enemy. We will not give up.

Sincerely,
The Pastor

From the Dog

Dear Listener,

I write this letter to you as pet who no longer lives. I gave my owner all kinds of signals, but he never understood me. I followed him everywhere he went when the kids were around. I know he thought it was because I was so attached. I was, but not for all the reasons he thought. You see when he left the room, that kid hit me with his fist. He threw me on the other dogs and tried to make me fight. He kicked me. He held my mouth closed so that I couldn't breathe. He tried to cut me with scissors. He always took my food. He put a pillow on me and tried to smoother me. I don't know what I did to this kid. I wish they would just take me to the pound. Either way, I am headed toward a same terminable end. Then it happened. My owner was leaving and he asked the kid to tie me up in the kennel. I remember that evil smirk like it was yesterday. He put my collar on me after my master got in the car, and then pulled it ever so tightly. I would have squealed, but it was too tight. My owner drove away and my heart raced. My breaths grew shorter and my eyes slowly shut in death. Finally the kid had killed me! I never asked for this. We were doing just fine. I didn't deserve this. I know my master would have never let this happen knowingly, but I think he was so sure of his own death that he missed mine. Animals aren't always the brightest, and we can be a little mischievous ourselves, but we know what love is. We understand good and bad, right and wrong. I just wish I could have had the opportunity to warn my master. He was nice.

Sincerely,
The Dog

P.S.

There is no true right or wrong answer to all the "fix its" for such occurrences. I do not claim to know all the answers, and I am by no means an expert. However, I know from experience that these families need their stories heard, their lives validated, and the simple opportunity of being fully heard without the worry of being judged, misunderstood, or labeled by the system, families, or professionals. The simplest means to bring peace to such confusion is to simply tell each persons side of the story uninterrupted, unadulterated, and uncensored. I hope that the opportunity to vent, understand and be understood provokes the action of healing for families involved in such times.

"Greater love hath no man than this than one who lays down his life for a friend." – Jn15:13

Printed in the United States
By Bookmasters